THE BLESSINGS AFTER

DIVORCE

by

CHERYLANN

SLYVESTER

All accounts and experiences in this book are true accounts as they were recalled by the author. All statements are from her own experience and thus her own words.

FOREWARD

When I first met CherylAnn, I will never forget the radiant smile on her face and the light of joy in her eyes. She was happy, joyous, and I could feel the presence of the Holy Spirit. My spirit connected to her immediately. She exemplified Nehemiah 8:10 – "… the joy of the Lord is your strength." I did not know at that time, she was a living witness of the fullness of that scripture, for the full verse states, "*Do not grieve*, for the joy of the Lord is your strength."

At that time, I did not know she was choosing daily to live out that powerful instruction from the Word of God. She was choosing not to suffer in prolonged grief. She was choosing to live in her purpose. She was choosing to move forward. She was choosing to enjoy the presence of the Lord Jesus, and live as the Bride of Christ. I did not know she had suffered betrayal, loss, infidelity, emotional abuse, rejection, the pain of broken marriages, and much more.

There were no traces of sadness, depression, or bitterness in her countenance. She was whole – made whole by the unconditional and unfailing love of Christ Jesus.

CherylAnn chose to love, and not hate, to move forward not stagnate, to heal and not stay wounded. CherylAnn was busily serving the Lord, building her businesses, enjoying family and friends, traveling the world, caring for others, and living life to the fullest. Yes, there is abundant life even after divorce! In these pages, you will read her inspiring story of overcoming difficult challenges to live in the fullness of her purpose and passion, a life fully dedicated and blessed by our Lord and Savior Jesus Christ.

Romans 8:28 tells us, "And we know that all things work together for good to those who love God, to those who are the called according to *His* purpose."

You will learn, by CherylAnn's powerful example, how to turn your test into a testimony, a mess into a message, and your pain into power. Our Heavenly Father is so gracious, kind, loving and powerful; He will turn any and ALL things that the devil means for evil to work out for your good! Joseph stated to his brothers upon their reconciliation in Genesis 50:20, "You intended to harm me, but God intended it for good to accomplish what is now being done, the saving of many lives."

What CherylAnn experienced in devastating betrayals, loneliness, and heartache, God has turned for the good, and now He is using this mighty vessel to save many women from discouragement, depression, and ultimate defeat. There is life after divorce!

There is no reason to stay stuck where you are! No matter what has happened, no matter what the circumstances look like, by receiving the love of Jesus, and allowing healing to permeate your life, your future will be beautiful, purposeful, and powerful. As CherylAnn will testify, Jesus will heal it ALL, and turn it for your good!

Isaiah 61:1-3, states "The Spirit of the Sovereign Lord is on me ... to comfort all who mourn, and provide for those who grieve in Zion— to bestow on them a crown of beauty instead of ashes, the oil of joy instead of mourning, and a garment of praise instead of a spirit of despair. They will be called oaks of righteousness, a planting of the Lord for the display of his splendor."

CherylAnn is a magnificent display of the Lord's splendor. She is a living, breathing, love letter from the Lord Jesus to all women who need to know His saving grace, unconditional love, and radical restoration. Let Him resurrect your dreams of love, liberation, and an overcoming life. She that the Son sets free is free indeed! It's time to begin again! Yes! There is LIFE - abundant life, overcoming life, purposeful life, the BLESSED life – after divorce!

She has experienced the fellowship of His sufferings, and now through her story, CherylAnn will show you the power of His resurrection. Receive the blessed life that Jesus has for you.

To God Be All the Glory!

The Power Coach™ Madeline Alexander

America's Premier Breakthrough Success Coach

www.ThePowerCoach.com

CHAPTER 1: SEBINA'S STORY

For 5 years, I experienced unnecessary struggle in my marriage—this should not have happened. I thought it would work, but looking back now, all the signs of trouble were there before I SAID I DO! Unlike most weddings, our day was not the happiest. A day intended to be a celebration of two people starting a new life together, declaring their commitment to one another for better or worse, in sickness and in health, until death do us part; however, our wedding day was sad to say the least.

Due to my lack of knowledge, I did not seek God about my mate nor did I get counsel on what a godly marriage should be; because of this, I experienced tremendous difficulty.

All marriages have difficulty; in fact, 1 Corinthians 7:28 warns us of them. However, if we understand covenant, commitment, and our fleshly nature, we are able to make wise choices and win in marriage. The key to a healthy marriage is the commitment to stay in God's presence. The Holy Spirit is the guide in directing and helping us choose the right mate.

My husband took a trip, while he was away, he connected with his former girlfriend. I was excited to pick him up from the airport when he returned, but that excitement soon turned to sadness after hearing his words. He informed me that he was really in love with this woman and she is who he wanted to be with—I was completely devastated. I felt like I lost my breath and my world was over; I felt betrayed by him and the other woman because we were married. How could this happen to me? Neither of them thought about my feelings in their decisions.

As time went on, the hurt intensified, they were communicating, and eventually he informed me of their plans to marry. Because I was a new Christian, I never shared my hurt or problems with anyone—even family. I felt God would turn this situation around and he would come back to me. One day, the Lord allowed my path to cross with the First Lady of a local church. I felt comfortable sharing my brokenness with her because I knew she would not judge me; she is still my mentor today. She married a virgin and still has a blessed union. She encouraged me to seek counseling and recommended a counselor.

CHAPTER 2

Jesus experienced pain, hurt, betrayal, and rejection; he understands what we feel and died so we can overcome a broken heart. The gospels of Matthew and Mark identify the place of prayer as Gethsemane—During Jesus agony as he prayed, drops of blood flowed down on his brow (Luke 22:44). In the end, Jesus accepts that the time has come for his betrayal. His acceptance of his assignment guaranteed our victory in situations of

betrayal—realizing this, I was able to take

steps toward my freedom.

> **Jesus Christ** experienced
> hematohidrosis while praying in
> the garden of Gethsemane before
> his crucification as mentioned in
> the Defenders Bible by Physician
> Luke as "and being in anguish he
> prayed more earnestly and his
> sweat was like drops of **blood**
> falling to the ground."

CHAPTER 3

While going through the pain, I received a lot of counseling—some of the counseling was not good and did not reflect godly principles. Thankfully, while attending beauty school, I met another amazing person named, Sharon Pearson. Sharon connected me with Pastor Motes who was a tremendous blessing. He offered regular counseling classes which were instrumental in my total healing from a broken heart. Within this process, the Lord sent so many pastors into my life to bless me because at that time I considered myself still a baby Christian, learning a lot of things that I never knew.

I encourage anyone reading this book to remove the shame and pride in your life. If you need to seek godly counsel—do it! I was in desperate need of help, and because I sought biblical counseling, my life changed for the better. If you are going through a divorce, consider seeking godly counseling; most importantly, get counseling before saying, "I Do!"

During my hurting period, I intentionally spent time reading scriptures and confessing them daily. Similar to the doctor ordering you to take pills three times a day to restore health, I followed this same method and quoted God's word each time I felt pain in my heart. For example, I would remind myself, I am the head and not the tail, I am above only and not beneath, I can do all things through Christ who strengthens me. I reminded myself of the purpose I have in Jesus—I knew one day the hurt I felt would pass. I believed these words and I sought God like never before because I wanted the pain to go away forever.

I do not wish the pain of divorce on anyone because it is similar to the pain of experiencing the death of a loved one. In the Old Testament, God instructed Moses to give the people a bill of divorce because the women at this time were treated so badly. This treatment was not God's original plan for men and women; he wants all of us to have a good experience with our mate and glorify him with our union and ministry. God's plan, is for a man and woman to separate only in death. I believe, if your husband dies, this is the only time you can decide to remarry or remain single and focus on the Lord—I do not believe God desires for us to have multiple partners because marriage is a sacred covenant between people.

The Names of God:

Yahweh – God is Constant
El Shaddai – God Almighty
Elohim – The Lord Most High
El Elyon – The Most High God
El Roi – The God Who Sees
Yahweh Yireh – The Lord Will Provide
Yahweh Nissi – The Lord is My Banner
Jehovah Rapha- The Lord My Healer
Yahweh Shalom – The Lord is Peace

Coming to the realization that I really had
to move out of the home I shared with my
husband was challenging. I moved into an
apartment with my daughter to embark on a
new journey. Although this journey was new,
and I was single, I decided to pursue options
for a home because I did not like the idea of
renting, and I wanted to raise my daughter in

a healthy environment. Also, I was accustomed to living in a home because of my Trinidadian values.

I began the journey of looking for a home—I was successful in my search and found a new one! This transition was great because my new home was one hour and fifteen minutes away from my previous location. At this point, I started my new business with the house I built from the ground up—life was good again. I still found myself struggling to remove the love I had for my husband from my heart and mind. Covenants are hard to break because of the connection and the soul tie.

CHAPTER 4

One night, I got tired of not being able to

sleep soundly; the heartache and pain would

wake me up all times of the night. So, I asked

a friend I trusted to pray with me because the

pain was something I could not take anymore.

My friend was married and did not understand

the extent of the pain I was experiencing;

nevertheless, she prayed for me. Although

God was blessing me, I still struggled with this

hurt—but after this night, I got up again and

the pain I felt previously vanished. The Holy Spirit, my comforter and healer, removed the pain! I give God all praise and thanks for the turning point I experienced that night—this type of pain finally left my life.

It is time for you to stop playing the victim and instead become the victor! Work through the areas you need to in your life so you can be ready for the next relationship. God desires us to be whole and complete in Christ Jesus—then we will complement our spouse.

Matthew 3:10, King James Version, says, "And now also the axe is laid unto the root of the trees: therefore every tree which bringeth not forth good fruit is hewn down and cast into the fire."

The following areas must be thrown into the fire:

1. Lack of financial discipline—poor stewardship

2. Lies

3. Inability to commit

4. Wandering eyes

5. Deception

6. Stealing

7. Not domesticated in the marriage

8. Dominating a mate

9. Dishonoring your husband or wife

10. Putting your spouse last and others first

11. Treating your spouse like a door mats

12. Not loving or respecting your spouse as Christ commanded

13. Pornography

14. Adultery

15.Gossip

Become the man or woman you were meant to be by working on yourself. Spend time in prayer, fast, exercise, and work out your own soul salvation. The commitment to this lifestyle will ensure success in your next relationship—you will not suffer lack because you will know who you are and can become the best you.

Allow God to wipe out all past memories, regardless of whatever has hurt you. He throws our sins into the sea of forgetfulness—

we can do this too by forgiving! Forgiveness is the key. We cannot focus on the hurt others have caused us; remember, we have not always acted our best either. Yet, God still forgives us and cleanses us. I implore you to forgive, forgive, forgive! Also, do not repeat past sins, go to God for the answer and seek Christian help to be free once and for all.

CHAPTER 5

Starting over was a great feeling; I moved into my

brand new home, opened a salon, made new friends—

my life was beginning again. At the church I began

attending, I met a brother who appeared to be a true

man of God. He was tall, handsome, and funny—the

complete package. We quickly became good friends

and eventually got engaged. Not too long after our

engagement, his true character was revealed. I found

out he was cheating on me our entire relationship—and

he had a baby with someone else. Surprisingly, before

his admittance, I dreamt he was leading a double life. I

am a firm believer that what is done in the dark, God will

allow it to come to light. Our relationship was totally

platonic, so I forgave, and we remained engaged. I

advised him to let the Pastors know of his infidelity to

get back in right standing. I had another dream about

this same guy; in this dream, he was disrespecting an

elderly lady. God kept revealing who this guy was

because he wanted to protect me. I was obedient to The

Holy Spirit after this dream, and decided to give the

engagement ring back. In this relationship, I learned,

you can still develop a soul tie with someone without

having sexual intercourse—this is not God's plan. I

thank God for helping me stay diligent by keeping my

eyes open before making a commitment in marriage;

this was a man led by lust and not by commitment.

Remember...lust takes--love gives. We must listen to

The Holy Spirit and allow Him to lead us into all truth. To

this day, I will not get involved with a man I do not have

peace about; I am committed to being a godly example

for other women by representing purity.

He was my friend, so I asked God to deliver him from the struggles he was experiencing. I wanted to see him become the man God intended him to be. We must continue to pray for our brothers and sisters even though their motives are not right. He was not my husband yet—he was my brother in Christ. The key in situations similar to this one is to stay alert, remain in God's presence, and do not settle because of loneliness. You are not alone because God is with you! In his presence is fullness of joy—he is the only one who can fill the void in your heart and give you true happiness. Giving back the engagement ring was not a

challenge for me—I am fulfilled in Christ!

Don't give your soul or heart away to just anyone.

Just as deception came to Eve in the garden, the devil

will attempt to trick us the same way. Do not fall for

flattery; wait to see if the person is bearing God's fruit—

be aware of counterfeits. God created Eve just for

Adam—he has the right person prepared for you. As

you wait, prepare yourself for marriage--it will have its

challenges. Determine in your heart to love and commit

to the person God sends.

The blessings after my divorce were a reflection of where I was. The hurt I experienced turned into the joy of the Lord!

The Holy Spirit has given me the peace that passes all understanding—it is difficult for people to comprehend. I am asked often, "Have you met anyone yet?" I reply, "God is preparing him for me, and he will find me in the right season."

The right person in the wrong season can end in disaster. If you wait on the right person and season—God is glorified, and you are blessed. In my previous marriage, I was ignorant of how a marriage should work and did not know the keys to make it successful. The

key is to be a team in your marriage; be vulnerable and

honest. Be open to godly counsel, commit to God, walk

in honesty, and glorify God.

Remain pure and do not sin against God. One of

the stories I reflect on often is that of Joseph. Potiphar's

wife attempted to seduce him daily (Genesis 39). Each

time, Joseph refused her because he did not want to sin

against God. We must learn from his example and

refuse to connect with people who are not meant for us.

Blessings are in our obedience.

CHAPTER 6: RELOCATION

Shortly after moving into my new home, with my

daughter, the Lord instructed me to move to Texas. I

knew absolutely nothing about Texas—I had never even

been. I shared God's instructions with friends, and they

thought I was crazy. Why build a brand new house and

sell it not too long after moving in?

I knew God spoke to me, so I no longer concerned

myself with the opinions of others. I learned then not to

share everything with everyone.

A client left a book by Juanita Bynum entitled, Walking

into Your Inheritance; I had to head to a meeting, so I

told her I would read the book while there. As I began to

read the book, the Lord continued to impress on my

heart to move to Texas. God spoke to Abraham the

same way in Genesis 12:1, he told him to leave his

country, family, to a land he would show him—he

promised to make him a great nation and make his

name great. God told him he would be a blessing and

his name would be great; those who cursed him would be cursed, and in him, all the families of the earth will be blessed.

God truly blessed my obedience—my home sold in record time. I arrived in early 2005, opened my salon in March, and bought my home in Texas in August. I began working hard to build my clientele. I had no connections in Texas, no family, so I had to go out and meet people to advertise my services. People started coming and referring others to visit my salon—the growth was amazing. The rental booths in my salon were filled quickly with other stylists. It was evident my obedience caused God to work miraculously in my life—

he sent me here to Texas for a purpose. I learned to be

patient, wait on the Lord, and listen to his leading. You

cannot be led by emotions or the opinions of others—

you must listen to God.

There are blessings after divorce—be patient and wait

on God's timing.

The season after the divorce was a time God wanted my

undivided attention. Never in my life was I so dedicated

to God. He connected me with the right people who

influenced me positively, encouraged my abilities, and

helped me to soar! I began to venture out and speak at

events, seminars, fashion shows, and more. Because of

my focus on God, doors of opportunity open for me. I

am confident, when the right time comes, God will send

my future husband, and I will know he is the one

because The Holy Spirit leads me into all truth. I may be

alone in Texas—but I am not lonely!

The reason I am not a lonely soul because I have been

restored to life by my creator. Psalms 23 says God

restores our soul and brings us to new life. I am growing

every day because I seek the things of God by staying

in his presence--my heart is full! There is no one who

can fill the place in my heart God reserves for himself.

After growing in the Lord more, I realized my husband had become an idol. When things got bad for me, all I could focus on was him and the hurt. God does not want us to have any other Gods before him. If we aren't careful, we can have idols in our lives and not realize it. Do not become so consumed with your spouse—trust only in the Lord.

Nuggets to Remember:

- No man or woman can satisfy the longing in your soul the way God can.

- No man or woman will treat you right if they only care about their wellbeing.

- Save yourself heartache and trouble by loving

  and treating yourself right first.

- Learn to forgive and move on when the man or

  woman cannot treat you the way you deserve.

The good news is—Christ has everything we need!

CHAPTER 7: LIFE AFTER A SPOUSE HAS DIED

The Story of Naomi & Ruth

Whether you have lost a spouse to death or divorce,

there is life on the other side of grief. An encouraging

story of life after loss is the one of Naomi and Ruth;

Ruth was Naomi's daughter-in-law. Ruth's husband,

Naomi's son, passes away along with Naomi's other son

and husband. Not only were they grieving this great

loss, but the land they were in was experiencing great

famine. Naomi encouraged Ruth to leave her and find

another husband, but she refused and said, "Don't ask

me to leave you and turn back. Wherever you go, I will

go; wherever you live, I will live. Your people will be my

people, and your God will be my God" (Ruth 1:16; New

Living Translation). Ruth's faithfulness to Naomi

catapulted them into blessings. Ruth ended up marrying

Boaz, a wealthy man, she gave birth to a child, and was

able to care for Naomi. I encourage you to read this

amazing story—it will encourage you. God will restore

your life just like he did for Ruth and Naomi!

Remember:

Favor is available to you!

Restoration is available to you!

A new family awaits you—Ruth gave birth to a child!

Grace is available to you!

God's love is for you!

Weeping may endure for a night—but joy comes in

the morning!

A new season awaits you!

Commitment and love awaits you!

Faithfulness awaits you!

A fulfilled life in Christ awaits you!

WAIT ON GOD!

CHAPTER 8: SEEKING LOVE AND

COMPANIONSHIP AFTER DIVORCE

After divorce, the temptation will come to rush into a

relationship. You must believe you are whole without a

companion. Loneliness can cause you to feel desperate!

The devil is always seeking someone he can devour, so

he attacks us at our vulnerable moments—do not fall

into his trap. We cannot conform to the standards or

opinions of the world when it comes to singleness.

I have seen many try and help God find their spouse;

often, they end up compromising their relationship with

God when they fall into sexual sin. The devil will send

people for short term gratification, but their intentions

are never good—they will use you and move on to the

next. Be careful of who you associate with, do not be

influenced by people who pressure you to find a new

companion at all costs. This dangerous practice will

cause you even more hurt in the process—it is like

practicing divorce. The world encourages people to

move from man to man or woman to woman, but this

should not be our behavior, because we are in this world

but we are not of it (John 17:16). Do not be moved by

loneliness—enjoy your time of singleness and live on

purpose! Participate in productive activities like;

traveling, repairing finances, learning a new skill, and

planning for your future!

God has a plan to prosper you in every area of life—this

will bring glory to His name! Proverbs 18:22 says, "He

who finds a wife, finds a good thing, and obtains favor

from the Lord" (King James Version). I encourage you to

focus on gaining godly friends—the best relationships

begin as friends first. Suppose, God wants you to wait

for 10 to 15 years before he sends a spouse; would you

be okay? Do you have the strength to wait or will you

focus on your biological clock? Many fear they will end

up too old to have children, but they fail to realize,

rushing into a marriage will bring your children into a

bad environment—wait on God. In my family, there are

several testimonies of women who had healthy babies

after forty; in fact, my Mother gave birth to my youngest

sister at 43. Trust God's promises for children!

The Bible says our body belongs to God—we are

fearfully, wonderfully, and beautifully made by God. He

will give you the desires of your heart. I asked God to

put his desires in my heart because I want to be filled by

Him. We must seek joy and happiness God's way and

not our way. Psalms 144:5 says, "happy are people

whose God is the Lord. If God is your main priority, you

will remain content. Our goal should be to live in the

fruits of the spirit! Embrace this chapter in your life by

staying busy, set goals and reach them—be a blessing

to others. God is doing a new thing in your life—it is time

for you to bloom!

Be the virtuous Proverbs 31 woman and flee fornication.

When we participate in sex outside of marriage, we are

slowly depleting our virtue and going against the will of

God. Maintain a high standard of being a virtuous

woman by keeping morals and integrity—this will ensure

you have strength and power for the work God desires

you to do. Pray and ask God to keep you alert to the

devil's schemes so you can hear His voice clearly. God

will show you the path to take; he will order your steps.

Flee fornication. Every sin that a man doeth is without the body; but he that committeth fornication sinneth against his own body. What? know ye not that your body is the temple of the Holy Ghost which is in you, which ye have of God, and ye are not your own? For ye are bought with a price: therefore glorify God in your body, and in your spirit, which are God's.
1 Corinthians 6:18-20

CHAPTER 9: LIVING WATER AFTER DIVORCE

John 14:1, speaks about the divine appointment

Jesus has with the Samaritan woman at the well. The

time was the sixth hour of the day which is typically very

warm. Jesus was thirsty and asked the woman at the

well for a drink. She reminded him Jews do not have

any communication or dealings with Samaritans—she

asked him, "Why do you want a drink from me?" Jesus

replies, "If you only knew the Gift God has for you and

who you are speaking to, you would ask me, and I

would give you living water" (John 4:10; New Living

Translation). The water Jesus desires to give us is a

spring of everlasting life. He wanted the Samaritan

woman to recognize who he was. Jesus then asks her

to go and call her husband; she informs him she does

not have one. Jesus already was aware of her past and

knew the man she was living with was not her husband.

This woman had five ex-husbands--she was desperately

after fulfillment. She reminds me of myself--I married

twice. My first marriage was at 23, and the other was at

29; in both situations, I was not led by God. After this

pain, I was in need of everlasting joy and life again—I

have it now! The living water Jesus brings is joy, peace,

and healing. You no longer have to live in pain and

rejection. I am certain this woman felt rejection because

of her many marriages, but Jesus opens her eyes to

true self-worth.

This encounter filled the woman with so much joy

and peace. Jesus did not judge the woman; he

understood her pain. He brings peace and joy—Jesus

restores! There is hope in Jesus if you stay in his

presence. You can see life differently and break free

from your past! Our sins are in the sea of forgetfulness.

After Jesus restores her, she shares with others in the

city. I am doing the same thing this woman did through

this book and every day.

My desire is for men and women who have

experienced divorce to come and receive living water

from God Almighty. Our Savior is not concerned with

what he have gone through; Jesus is knocking on the

door of our heart offering everlasting life. Once I let

Jesus in, my desires became his; I no longer feel

pressure to date like I did once before. Believe in

Jesus—he will give you strength! Maybe you are

divorced with children—he will sustain you and be a

father to them and direct you. Find a church home and a

support team to give you direction. Look for godly

relatives and friends to help you raise your children

instead of jumping into another relationship. Jesus is

there for you! Become involved in a church; get busy

working in ministry.

Our latter days will be greater than our former days.

Remember, Our latter days are greater than our former

days. Remember, Jesus was rejected, but he became

the head cornerstone (Psalms 118:22). Bad things

happen, but we overcome! People will hear your

testimony and find strength and encouragement. Jesus

forgives us no matter what we have done.

God has given me a successful career as a

cosmetologist—I love my work with all my heart and

soul. I enjoy meeting people and telling them about the

living water Jesus provides. Our diligence to wait on

God will inspire others to do the same. Give Jesus your

worship, praise, possessions, heart, soul, and body. You

will be a blessing to his people and to The Body of

Christ.

Let your light shine—flow in the anointing God has

given you. Heal the brokenhearted! Jesus chose the

woman at the well, not because she was perfect; he

chose her because he wanted to change her life. Allow

him to change your life, too.

CHAPTER 10: INHERITANCE

The reason I never stopped building my life is because

of my daughter, Lateefah Roberts.

The Bible instructs us to leave an inheritance for our children

and grandchildren. Although I was now on my own after the

divorce, I decided to keep growing, pushing, living, pursuing

to be the best me I can. I am determined to fulfill my purpose on the earth. I want to leave a lasting legacy for my daughter

and nieces and nephews.

I always knew I had to be strong for my child because I did

not want to pass down negative behavior. I told myself, "You

cannot crumble!" I wanted my daughter to know how to stand

on the Word of God when trials and tribulations come into

your life. I taught her to know God will never leave nor

forsake us (Hebrews 13:5). I also taught her the race is not

given to the swift but to those who will endure until the end.

Lastly, I taught her God is only moved by our faith.

I am very grateful for Lateefah Roberts because she stood

with me in hard and dark times. We always have stuck

together and sacrificed for one another. Everything I do is for

her! I give God all praise and thanks for my daughter because

she loves me unconditionally—she is my greatest blessing

and the star in my life.

<u>CHAPTER 11 DON'T REPEAT THE SAME MISTAKES</u>

In Genesis 2:7, God breathed the breath of life into

Adam's nostrils—the power of God. He put Adam into a

deep sleep and took a rib out of him to create Eve. Allow

God to prepare the man you desire; leave him in his

deep sleep until God breathes into his soul. He will

come at the appropriate time.

When the right man's eyes behold you, he will know you

are the one—the two will become one flesh. You both

will walk together in unity because that is God's plan. Be

patient. Allow God to work on your behalf. God will send

a man with his power, purpose, and life of God. He will

possess the fruits of the spirit and the standards of God.

If you do not wait on God, you will end up in frustration

trying to fix a person in your own strength. Do not get

hooked up, yoked up, or in bondage with the wrong

person—you will waste time and virtue. Once we were

sinners, but when we accepted Jesus as our Lord and

Savior, he breathed into us the breath of life. We must

walk, talk, and live differently because of the power of

God in our life.

Determine to be like Esther; she continued in

preparation for 12 months before going to meet the

King. Do not waste time on men who do not have the

power or presence of God in their lives. You need a

mate who will encourage you to walk in the light of

God's ways. He will be your leader, protector, provider,

and example. He will bless, respect, cultivate,

encourage, love you unconditionally, and raise your

standards higher to be like the Proverbs 31 woman.

Ladies, it is time to set goals! No matter your age,

determine to get prepared for your next season—

whether it means being single or married. Always desire

the best!

CHAPTER 12:THE BLESSED LIFE AFTER DIVORCE

There is hope after divorce. Love God, be dedicated and

disciplined—worship, praise, and pray. Love yourself

and take care of your body, mind, and spirit by

exercising, fasting, and forgiving. Appreciate who you

are and live in expectation; set 5-10 year goals for

yourself and reach them. God has people he is raising

up to bless and direct you! Write down your visions,

achieve your goals, and help others. God has great

plans for you! Do not be anxious but give God praise

and thanks. Our diligence to live in excellence by

avoiding procrastination will be a blessing to the

generations after us. God wants us to be a

representation of Him in the world!

Closing Prayer

I, CherylAnn Sylvester, pray The Holy Spirit ministers to

your heart, soul, and spirit throughout the pages of this

book. I pray you will transform and become a new

person in Jesus. I pray every burden you have is

removed instantly in Jesus name and by His power. I

pray for healing for broken hearts, sickness, anxiety,

hurt, abandonment, abuse, and degradation. I pray the

weapons the devil has thrown will not prevail. You are

free right now in the name of Jesus! Believe you are free

now—faith is now! Live free and blessed in Jesus

Name, Amen!

Matthew 6:33 New International Version (NIV)

33 But seek first his kingdom and his righteousness, and

all these things will be given to you as well.

TESTIMONIALS

When God called my husband home, I didn't know what to do; but, I remembered Psalms 28:6, "Blessed be the Lord, because he has heard the voice of my supplications" (King James Version). In verses 7-8, it says, "The Lord is my strength and my shield; my heart trusted in him, and I am helped: therefore my heart greatly rejoiceth; and with my song will I praise him" (King James Version). Without the strength of the Lord, I would not have made it. My advice to anyone who has lost a loved one is to stand on the word and depend on God—he is the answer!

-Dr. Bettye Morgan

My name is LW, and I have been married for 26 years. As a young Christian, approaching adulthood, I remember attending women's Sunday school classes centered on becoming a godly wife. After years of being attentive during these lessons, I felt equipped with everything I needed to be a wife pleasing to God and my future husband.

At the time, I was not dating anyone; I was in nursing school and still living at home with my parents. In my second semester of nursing school, I met a man who instantly swept me off my feet. He had just returned home from serving in the Marines—he was handsome, funny, charming, sweet, tough, and accomplished—he was unlike anyone I had met before. The more we spent time together, the more convinced I became he was the one for me. I made it my mission to get him to church so he could receive the same teachings I was receiving. I wanted him to have the knowledge and ability to be a good husband. Unfortunately, there were no classes or consistent teaching for young men to learn how to become a good husband. I made sure, however; we were diligent in attending Sunday, mid-week, and young adult services.

After a year and a half of dating, we were married, and it was time to put all we learned into practice. I did not know what to expect going into marriage, but I believed if we remained in the Word of God, we could experience bliss! Also, I believed, there was nothing my husband and I could not overcome together as long as we kept God in our marriage. Not only was I naïve, I was in for a rude awakening.

After being married for a few years, I realized nothing in the world could have prepared me for what I experienced as a Christian wife. The many trials and tribulations caused me to question God which lead me to make bad decisions. I started to try and fix situations myself rather than yielding to God.

My father always told me this, "There is something good in every situation—you just have to look for it." He also would tell me, "You can handle situations two ways— with God or without Him. After hearing this a few times, I realized he was right, and I changed my outlook; I began to look at everything differently. Rather than having a defeated approach to my life and marriage, I reminded myself of God's goodness and blessings. Also, I resolved, to never forget God is always working on our behalf. His word says in Romans 8:28, "All things work together for good to them that love God, to them who are called according to his purpose." This passage reminds me over and over, no matter how bad or hopeless things may appear, God has a plan for me if I can always trust and depend on Him. Another valuable lesson I learned over the years is to focus on myself. It is very easy to focus on what your husband or wife isn't doing. When we take the focus off of the other person and place it on ourselves instead, we can work on self-improvement. This will result in us becoming more tolerable and understanding of one another. Thank you, CherylAnn, for the opportunity to share a few words in your book. I love you dearly and pray this book will bless all who read it.

-LW

Life Lessons of a Divorcee

When I was a single young adult, I found myself many nights falling asleep with my Bible on my pillow as I cried out to God, "Please Father, send me a husband." This need for a husband was a common cry because those days I felt empty and lost as I frequently compared myself to countless others who appeared to be happy and complete. I didn't even know who I was as a woman. I was not aware of the role and duties of a wife. Needless to say, I couldn't even imagine what a husband represented. All I know was that I wanted one. There were many false starts in my attempts to find "the one"—too many honestly. A piece of my soul left with each of them creating a gaping hole in my spiritual walk. Yes, I was a professed Christian and serving God the entire time with many of "the older saints" looking on with no directions. I imagine that they recognized the anointing of God on my life and assumed that I had it all together. I didn't. I was lonely, afraid, secretive and lost, yet, I continued my quest to be married.

Skipping ahead after several failed relationships, "the one" seemed to appear out of nowhere. This had to be God. He was the ideal. As time went on, I found myself vacillating between prayers of thanksgiving, and nights

of tears and doubt. I cried, "Father, did I hear You"?
With some maturity under my belt , I began to look at
myself. For the first time in my adult life, I began to see
myself as God saw me. I was finally able to understand
what the tools to a successful marriage looked like and
was ready to use them. It takes two. Unfortunately, that
marriage ended in divorce. I say, unfortunately, because
we were two broken people attempting to make each
other whole. After two months of separation, my then
husband asked for a divorce, and I granted it. His
request created the type of devastation that I couldn't
imagine surviving—but I did. With God's help, I did.
My tears became my closest companions as I allowed
my broken heart to be vulnerable in God's capable
healing hands. I woke up one morning laughing
uncontrollably as I looked at my Bible once again lying
next to me in bed as "The One." God's loving presence
and instructions to me were lifesaving. He instructed me
to get wisdom, gain understanding and offer Grace. I
had to learn to tell the story without blaming. I spoke
grace to the situation and everyone involved and as I
expressed heartfelt grace in my prayers and to all who
inquired of my failed marriage my God healed my heart.

And just like that, the deep, empty, and loveless chasm in my heart were filled. I forgave the relationships of the past, and I forgave myself. I learned that I was contributing to the suffering of my now ex-husband when I demanded from him what I was not willing or able to give to myself. Each time I gave grace I received a lost piece of my soul as the exchange. The tears you ask? They are now tears of joy. I am no longer a slave to fear…. I am a child of God. Single but not alone.

- Patti Denise Henry

LOVE AND COMMITMENT

Marriage can be a lifelong commitment--my brother, Reynold Sylvester, and his wife, Sharon Sylvester are living proof. In 2019, they celebrate 29 years of marriage! They fell in love as teenagers and remained together. I have great admiration for them because they are best friends. One of the formulas for their successful marriage is selflessness and sacrifice. They consistently give and sacrifice for one another—they are true examples! My brother and sister-in-law are in their early fifties now and still have joy and love together. They do not allow anything to interfere with their union; their love for one another is unconditional. They share a lovely daughter named, Renea Sylvester who is now 30 years old—she is the joy of their heart.

Scriptural References

Love

1 Corinthians 13:4-8 New International Version (NIV)

4 Love is patient, love is kind. It does not envy, it does not boast, it is not proud. **5** It does not dishonor others, it is not self-seeking, it is not easily angered, it keeps no record of wrongs. **6** Love does not delight in evil but rejoices with the truth. **7** It always protects, always trusts, always hopes, always perseveres.

8 Love never fails. But where there are prophecies, they will cease; where there are tongues, they will be stilled; where there is knowledge, it will pass away.

Peace

Philippians 4:6 New International Version (NIV)

6 Do not be anxious about anything, but in every situation, by prayer and petition, with thanksgiving, present your requests to God.

Forgiveness

Matthew 6:14 New International Version (NIV)

14 For if you forgive other people when they sin against you, your heavenly Father will also forgive you.

Joy

John 16:24 New International Version (NIV)

24 Until now you have not asked for anything in my name. Ask and you will receive, and your joy will be complete.

Reconciliation

2 Corinthians 5:18 New International Version (NIV)

18 All this is from God, who reconciled us to himself through Christ and gave us the ministry of reconciliation.

Healing

Isaiah 53:5 New International Version (NIV)

5 But he was pierced for our transgressions,

   he was crushed for our iniquities;

the punishment that brought us peace was on him,

   and by his wounds we are healed.

Rejection

Matthew 21:42 New International Version (NIV)

42 Jesus said to them, "Have you never read in the Scriptures:

"'The stone the builders rejected

   has become the cornerstone;

the Lord has done this,

   and it is marvelous in our eyes?

New Heart

Ezekiel 36:26 New International Version (NIV)

26 I will give you a new heart and put a new spirit in you; I will remove from you your heart of stone and give you a heart of flesh.

Restoration for the Soul

Psalm 23:3 New International Version (NIV)

3　he refreshes my soul.

He guides me along the right paths

　for his name's sake.

Trusting God

Psalm 91:2 New International Version (NIV)

2 I will say of the LORD, "He is my refuge and my fortress,

　my God, in whom I trust."

MEET THE AUTHOR

CherylAnn Sylvester

Made in the USA
Columbia, SC
23 May 2019